Help Ha...

Contents	Page
Where Hawaiian Monk Seals live	2-3
Why are the seals in danger?	4-5
Seals and fishermen	6-7
What seals eat	8-9
Bad things for seals	10-11
People can help the seals	12-15
Save Hawaiian Monk Seals	16

written by L.J. Welsh

Hawaiian Monk Seals live only in Hawaii. They are not found in any other place on Earth.

Now there are only 1,300 of them left. There were a lot more 50 years ago. They are in big danger.

Fishermen have lived with the seals for hundreds of years. They know that the seals need to be looked after. They call them "sea dogs".

If they all died, there would never be any of these seals in the world again.

Fishermen in Hawaii want to find out how to help these seals. Sometimes hungry seals take fish from the fishing lines. If the seal swallows a hook, it could kill the seal.

The fishermen want to learn ways to keep the seals safe. They can use new hooks that don't kill the seals.

looking for food

Hawaiian Monk Seals look for good things to eat in the sea.
Some of the things that they like are: crabs, octopuses, eels, shrimps, lobsters, and small fish.

dinner time

Some things are bad for the seals. They can't always find all the food they need to eat. Then they get hungry, and they swim into fishing nets. Sometimes big sharks catch them and eat them.

People must not come too close or make too much noise. They need to keep away. The seals need to sleep and look after their babies.

mother and baby

We can all help to keep the Hawaiian Monk Seals from going extinct. The first thing is to learn about these seals. We can let people know how the seals are in danger.

sleeping

People who go fishing in Hawaii can use hooks that won't be bad for the seals. They can keep away from seals on the beach to let them sleep or play.
Let's help these seals!